Dear Parent:

Congratulations! Your child is taking the first steps on an exciting journey. The destination? Independent reading!

STEP INTO READING® will help your child get there. The program offers five steps to reading success. Each step includes fun stories and colorful art. There are also Step into Reading Sticker Books, Step into Reading Math Readers, Step into Reading Write-In Readers, Step into Reading Phonics Readers, and Step into Reading Phonics First Steps! Boxed Sets—a complete literacy program with something for every child.

Learning to Read, Step by Step!

Ready to Read   Preschool–Kindergarten
• big type and easy words • rhyme and rhythm • picture clues
For children who know the alphabet and are eager to begin reading.

Reading with Help   Preschool–Grade 1
• basic vocabulary • short sentences • simple stories
For children who recognize familiar words and sound out new words with help.

Reading on Your Own   Grades 1–3
• engaging characters • easy-to-follow plots • popular topics
For children who are ready to read on their own.

Reading Paragraphs   Grades 2–3
• challenging vocabulary • short paragraphs • exciting stories
For newly independent readers who read simple sentences with confidence.

Ready for Chapters   Grades 2–4
• chapters • longer paragraphs • full-color art
For children who want to take the plunge into chapter books but still like colorful pictures.

STEP INTO READING® is designed to give every child a successful reading experience. The grade levels are only guides. Children can progress through the steps at their own speed, developing confidence in their reading, no matter what their grade.

Remember, a lifetime love of reading starts with a single step!

To Caffery Garff—J.C.
To Ted—P.W.

www.stepintoreading.com

Educators and librarians, for a variety of teaching tools, visit us at
www.randomhouse.com/teachers

Library of Congress Cataloging-in-Publication Data
Cole, Joanna.
Hungry, hungry sharks / by Joanna Cole ; illustrated by Patricia Wynne.
  p.   cm. — (Step into reading. A step 3 book)
Originally published: New York : Random House, c1986.
SUMMARY: A simple discussion of the kinds of sharks and their behavior.
ISBN 0-394-87471-4 (pbk.) — ISBN 0-394-97471-9 (lib. bdg.)
1. Sharks—Juvenile literature. [1. Sharks.]
I. Wynne, Patricia, ill. II. Title. III. Series: Step into reading. Step 3 book.
QL638.9 .C59 2003 597.3—dc21 2002014521

Printed in the United States of America   59 58 57 56 55

Hungry, Hungry SHARKS

by Joanna Cole
illustrated by Patricia Wynne

Random House 🏠 New York

Millions and millions
of years ago,
the earth did not look
the way it does now.
Strange-looking plants
grew in swamps.
Reptiles with wings
flew in the air.

Everywhere on land were
dinosaurs, dinosaurs, dinosaurs.

Out at sea

there were strange creatures too.

Some looked like dragons.

Some looked like fish.

This big fish

could swim very fast.

It had sharp teeth

and a big fin on its back.

What kind of fish was this?

A shark!

There are no more
dinosaurs left on earth.
But there are still
plenty of sharks.

thresher

tiger shark

angel shark

Today there are more than
three hundred kinds of sharks.

basking shark

black-tipped
reef shark

sand shark

oceanic white-tipped
shark

Port Jackson's
shark

Not all sharks are big.
Many, many kinds
are less than three feet long.

The dwarf shark is no bigger
than your hand.

The small carpet shark lies

on the ocean floor

like a rug.

The leopard shark has spots.

It grows to be about four feet long.

The biggest shark

is the whale shark.

It is longer than a bus.

The whale shark

has three thousand teeth.

But it will never bite you.

It eats only tiny

shrimp and fish.

The whale shark is very gentle.
A diver can even hitch a ride
on its back.

These are blue sharks.

They are far out at sea

hunting for food.

Suddenly

they pick up

the smell of blood.

The sharks speed up.

They shoot through the water

like torpedoes.

In a few minutes

they find a dead whale.

The blue sharks tear off

big chunks of whale meat.

Now the water is

full of biting sharks.

If one shark gets hurt,

the others turn on it.

They will eat that shark too.

In a short time

the whale is all gone.

The sharks swim away.

Nothing is left.

Nothing but bones.

Blue sharks are called
the wolves of the sea.
This is because
they stay together in packs.
Blue sharks often swim
after a ship for days.
A long time ago
sailors thought this meant that
someone was going to die.

Why do blue sharks
really follow ships?
The sharks come
because of noises
from the ship.
Then they stay to eat
garbage that is thrown
into the water.

The most dangerous shark

in the sea

is the great white shark.

It is named after

its white belly.

The teeth of the great white shark
are big and sharp.

Very, very sharp.

It can eat a whole seal
in one bite.

The great white shark is
the size of a speedboat.

This great white shark

has just had babies.

Most fish lay eggs.

But most sharks do not.

Their babies are born alive.

A baby shark is called a pup.

The pup of the great white shark

is almost the size of a man.

As soon as they are born

the pups go their own way.

It is not safe to stay

near a hungry mother.

The baby sharks swim off
to catch their own food.
One eats a fish.
Another gets a crab.
The pups had better
watch out for puffer fish.

The puffer fish can blow up
like a balloon.
If a shark eats it,
its spines get stuck
in the shark's throat.
The shark will die.

Not many animals

can kill great white sharks.

The stingray

flaps through the sea

like a giant bat.

Its tail has a poison stinger.

The poison can kill most animals.

But a great white shark

can eat a stingray—

stinger and all!

The swordfish is
a very strong fish.
It can cut and stab
with its long nose.
But even a swordfish
almost always loses a fight
with a great white shark.

Another big shark is

the hammerhead shark.

It is easy to see

how it got its name.

Like other big sharks,

the hammerhead never sleeps

and never stops swimming.

Most fish have air balloons

inside them.

But sharks do not.

If they stop swimming,

they sink.

This hammerhead swims
to a group of dolphins.
It tries to catch
one of the young dolphins.
But sharks do not always
get their way.
The dolphins fight back.

One dolphin dives

under the water.

It comes up and

hits the hammerhead.

The shark flies up

in the air.

It falls back on the water.

SMACK!

The dolphins keep
hitting the shark.
After a while
the shark stops moving.
It sinks down into the water.
It is dead.

Dolphins are smart animals.

They can work together

to kill an enemy.

But sharks are not as smart.

They have tiny brains.

A shark's brain is small.

But its teeth are big.

It has many rows of teeth.

When a tooth breaks off,

a new tooth moves up

to take its place.

A shark uses up thousands

of teeth every year!

What do sharks eat
with all these teeth?
Fish and more fish.
Other sharks.
Seals,
turtles,
crabs.
Almost anything
that swims in the sea.

Sometimes sharks eat

things that are not food.

No one knows why.

All these things

have been found

inside big sharks:

a wallet,

a fur coat,

a drum,

a bottle of wine,

a chest of jewels,

a barrel of nails,

and a suit of armor!

Do sharks eat people?

Yes, they do.

If a person is near a big shark,

the shark may attack.

But the number of people
killed by sharks
is very small.
More people die
from bee stings
than from shark bites!

Sharks do not
go hunting for people.
But people do
go hunting for sharks.
Some people like to go
fishing for sharks.
They have to be careful.
A shark may look dead.
Then all at once
it can "wake up"—
and bite!

43

Scientists want to study sharks.

But it is hard

to study them at sea.

And it is hard to keep

big sharks alive in a tank.

Once scientists caught

a great white shark.

They put it in a tank

with other fish.

But the shark did not eat.

And it kept bumping into

the sides of the tank.

After a few days

the shark began to die.

So the scientists

took the shark back to sea.

They set it free.

There are many things

we do not know about sharks.

We do not know

how long sharks live.

Or how much food

a shark has to eat

to stay alive.

But we do know that sharks

are here to stay.

They are fast and strong.

They hardly ever get sick.

And there is always

plenty of food for them.

As long as there are oceans,

there will be sharks.